DATE DUE		OCT 0 2
GAYLORD			PRINTED IN U.S.A.

The Mystery Library

Dragons

Michael J. Wyly

Lucent Books, Inc.
10911 Technology Place, San Diego, California 92127

On cover: The Dragon of Wantley

Library of Congress Cataloging-in-Publication Data

Wyly, Michael J., 1970–
    Dragons / by Michael J. Wyly.
        p. cm. — (The mystery library)
    Includes bibliographical references and index.
        Summary: Discusses what a dragon is, dragon's breath,
    guardians, dragon slayers, and the role of dragons in myth, fan-
    tasy, art, and literature.
        ISBN 1-56006-972-4 (hardback : alk. paper)
        1. Dragons—Juvenile literature. [1. Dragons.] I. Title. II.
    Mystery library (Lucent Books)
        GR830.D7 W95 2002
        398 '.469—dc21   2001002790

Copyright 2002 by Lucent Books, Inc.
10911 Technology Place, San Diego, California 92127

Printed in the U.S.A.

Contents

Foreword

In Shakespeare's immortal play, *Hamlet*, the young Danish aristocrat Horatio has clearly been astonished and disconcerted by his encounter with a ghost-like apparition on the castle battlements. "There are more things in heaven and earth," his friend Hamlet assures him, "than are dreamt of in your philosophy."

Many people today would readily agree with Hamlet that the world and the vast universe surrounding it are teeming with wonders and oddities that remain largely outside the realm of present human knowledge or understanding. How did the universe begin? What caused the dinosaurs to become extinct? Was the lost continent of Atlantis a real place or merely legendary? Does a monstrous creature lurk beneath the surface of Scotland's Loch Ness? These are only a few of the intriguing questions that remain unanswered, despite the many great strides made by science in recent centuries.

Lucent Books' Mystery Library series is dedicated to exploring these and other perplexing, sometimes bizarre, and often disturbing or frightening wonders. Each volume in the series presents the best-known tales, incidents, and evidence surrounding the topic in question. Also included are the opinions and theories of scientists and other experts who have attempted to unravel and solve the ongoing mystery. And supplementing this information is a fulsome list of sources for further reading, providing the reader with the means to pursue the topic further.

The Mystery Library will satisfy every young reader's fascination for the unexplained. As one of history's greatest scientists, physicist Albert Einstein, put it:

> The most beautiful thing we can experience is the mysterious. It is the source of all true art and science. He to whom this emotion is a stranger, who can no longer wonder and stand rapt in awe, is as good as dead: his eyes are closed.

Of Might and Mystery

There he lay, a vast red-gold dragon, fast asleep. . . . Beneath him, under all his limbs and his huge coiled tail, and about him on all sides stretching away across unseen floors, lay countless piles of precious things, gold wrought and unwrought, gems and jewels, and silver red-stained in the ruddy light.

The Hobbit by J. R. R. Tolkien

Probably no animal in the world, real or imaginary, has inspired the modern imagination as much the dragon. Popular novels like *The Hobbit* by J. R. R. Tolkien reveal this mysterious beast in a terrible light describing vicious fire-breathing lizards, sometimes hundreds of feet long, that hoard vast treasures and punish mercilessly all who would try to steal them. Other depictions, like those of the fantasy novelist Anne McCaffrey portray the dragon as an ally to humans. And films such as *Dragonheart* portray the dragon as terrible to behold as well as friendly toward humankind.

The stories are not new, however. In fact, evidence of humankind's fascination with the dragon is as old as recorded history. Chinese manuscripts describing the appearance and behavior of the dragon date back as far as the twenty-seventh century B.C. Ancient Greek mythology describes numerous dragons: some, like the Hydra, have multiple heads; others live within the darkest depths of the ocean. One of the earliest examples of English literature, the eighth-century epic *Beowulf* devotes more than nine hundred lines to the description of a great and furious dragon. Indeed, drawings and descriptions of this fabled beast and its behavior abound everywhere from the earliest literatures of western Europe, the art and history of China and Japan, and the ancient religions of Greece.

What is most striking is that although the descriptions range over vast distances and through so many eras of history, the dragon is nearly always identifiable because, for the most part, it possesses the same appearance. Nearly all ancient literatures, histories, and mythologies seem to have this one beast in common. As scholar Grafton Elliot Smith explains:

> This composite wonder-beast ranges from Western Europe to the Far East of Asia, and . . . also even across the Pacific to America. . . . But it is not merely a case of structural or anatomical similarities, but also of psychological identity, that clinches the proof of the derivation of this fantastic brood

Dragonheart's dragon-slaying knight, played by Dennis Quaid, encounters a dragon that is both terrible and friendly.

from the same parents. Wherever the dragon is found, it displays a social partiality for weather. It controls the rivers or the seas, dwells in pools or wells, or in the clouds on the tops of mountains, regulates the tides, the flow of streams, or the rainfall, and is associated with thunder and lightning. Its home is a mansion at the bottom of the sea, where it guards vast treasures, usually pearls, but also gold and precious stones. In other instances, the dwelling is upon the top of a high mountain; and the dragon's breath forms the rain-clouds.[1]

Historians and other specialists of dragon lore have sought to explain these similarities. In the course of their investigations, each has had to confront the key question that unites the research: How could so many cultures—which are noted for their differences as much as their similarities—share this very specific and fabulous creature?

Many historians have pointed at the physical differences that *do* exist in order to show that the similarities are the product of coincidence. For example, the dragons of China possess antlers instead of ears while the dragons of Europe may possess no visible ears at all. They then explain how the differences in appearance relate to the variety of roles the dragon played in these cultures. The antlers of the Chinese dragon, for instance, are related to the Chinse belief that the dragon possesses the attributes of other animals (in this case, the deer) that are important to the Chinese culture; likewise, the European dragon's lack of ears is based on its relationship with the biblical snake, a creature noted for its evil intent and identified with Satan. In so doing, the historians have found that different cultures have relied upon the image of the dragon in varied and often contradicting fashions.

Because of differences like these, historians typically divide the types of dragons into two major categories: the

Western variety, meaning dragons of European and Middle East origins; and the Eastern variety, meaning those dragons whose origins lie in China, Japan, Taiwan, and Korea. Many historians argue that there is little connection between the two varieties. Or, they argue, if there is a connection, it is an old one upon which individual cultures have built over time to create dragons with unique functions that still retain certain similar characteristics.

Despite these differences, the similarities in description and behavior remain overwhelming. Indeed, the consistency with which the dragon is represented has prompted some researchers to ask whether another, more obvious explanation exists. In other words, could the dragon have actually existed? Skeptics point out that absolutely no archaeological evidence exists to support such an idea. Yet other evidence does suggest that ancient peoples believed in the existence of these mighty beasts. Evidence like this leaves researchers wondering what reasons these people could have had for believing in a dragon if it did not exist. Why are there so many recorded accounts—both historical as well as fictive?

The search for the answers to these questions spans the globe. And the hunt for the truth behind this most mysterious of beasts is one which seems to unite most major world cultures.

Chapter 1

What Is the Dragon?

What does the average dragon look like? What does it do? Given the profound lack of direct evidence with respect to the existence of the dragon, historians have had to turn to other sources in their efforts to answer these questions. Although archaeological evidence of the dragon has never been unearthed, numerous historical and literary testimonies do exist that describe the dragon, its behavior, and where it might have lived. From similarities found within these examples, historians have been able to construct an accurate picture of the "average" dragon while also showing some of the basic differences between its Eastern and Western varieties.

Depictions of the Dragon

The most common feature of the dragon is its serpentine or lizardlike appearance. Like a lizard, the dragon typically has four legs, at the end of which are sharp, curved claws. It has both a tail and long neck. Its head and mouth, too, are lizardlike, and in some descriptions the dragon may have horns that protrude from the top of its head. Its jaws are filled with teeth or fangs capable of rending apart the flesh of its prey or a potential enemy. In many descriptions, the dragon also possesses a forked tongue, which it flickers on occasion as if testing the wind. The dragon is covered in scales that provide it with an armorlike protection. Its unblinking, snakelike eyes are said to close rarely—if ever— and to glitter menacingly even in the remotest of light.

Another trait consistent among most descriptions of dragons is their ability to take flight. Unlike the lizard or the snake, the dragon is usually said to possess wings mounted to its back with which it can fly—although this is truer of the Western dragons than of their Eastern counterparts. In Western traditions, the wings are typically

Dragons, such as this one on a hotel sign in Germany, are often depicted with four legs; sharp, curved claws; jaws with fangs; and wings with skin stretched over the skeletal riblike wing framework.

depicted as stretched skin over a skeletal, riblike framework, similar to those of a bat. Occasionally, however, dragons may also possess feathers. In Eastern traditions, the wings are always feathered, and even Eastern dragons that do not possess wings still have the ability to fly.

These consistencies certainly intrigue historians because they suggest that consistent imagery of the dragon was somehow available to various cultures separated by vast geographical distances. However, given that smaller animals, like lizards or birds, exist all over the globe, a dragon's lizardlike appearance or the existence of wings would not necessarily be enough to arouse scholarly interest. But a number of other similarities exist, in particular the dragon's horrific size, form, and powers.

The Dragon's Breath

Although the sheer sight of the dragon may seem frightening enough to scare off even the bravest defenders, perhaps the most impressive aspect of the dragon is also the most cited and feared—its breath. In both European and Asian traditions, the breath of the dragon plays a vital role in the creature's behavior and imposing nature. However, although both Eastern and Western cultures attribute a breath weapon to the dragon, the exact nature of this ability differs substantially between the two traditions.

In Western representations, the might of the dragon's breath is alternately described as poisonous or fiery—sometimes even both. In either form, the breath is indeed a terrible force. Examples of the dragon breathing streams of fire abound in Western literature. One of the oldest and best-known literary descriptions is in the Old English epic *Beowulf*. In the final sections of the saga, the destructive force of the dragon's breath is detailed as the dragon terrorizes the countryside in revenge for the theft of a piece of its treasure, a jeweled cup:

The monster, swelling with exasperation, impatiently waited for the night to fall, when the theft of the cup could be repaid with fire. To the delight of the Worm [the dragon], the day drew to a close. It had no wish to stay in the tumulus [its caves], but flashed forth armed with flame. . . . The creature began to spew fire and burn dwellings; and while the light of burning filled the people with horror, the flying monster spared no living thing. . . . Before daybreak, it flew back to its secret home, the treasure-hoard, having surrounded the country-folk with fire and flame and burning.[2]

The poisonous, fiery breath of the dragon, as depicted in an eighteenth-century engraving, is an important feature in both Western and Eastern cultures.

But fire is not the only breath weapon ascribed to the dragon. Other Western traditions describe dragons that can exhale a cloud of powerful and lethal poison with which they engulf their enemies. Such was the case with a dragon confronted by the legendary Moslem, Jewish, and Christian saint, El Khudr—whom the Christians call Mar Jiryis. According to all three religious traditions, this dragon occupied a spring near the modern-day city of Beirut and would not allow anyone near the water source. When some of the local warriors attempted to attack the dragon to drive it off or kill it, each of the warriors was slain as the dragon belched a venomous cloud at its would-be adversaries. According to the story, it was not until much later, with the successful onslaught of El Khudr, which resulted in the death of the dragon, that the people were once again able to use the spring.

Of Dragons and Storms

Eastern traditions also attribute impressive properties to the dragon's breath, although it is never described as fiery or poisonous. Instead, the breath of the Eastern dragon is always associated with water, lightning, or a foglike mist. Typically, the Eastern dragon, when angered, uses its supernatural breath to cause storm clouds to form in the sky, thereby summoning horrific rains and lightning storms that can lay the countryside to waste because of resulting floods and erosion.

One well-known example of an angry dragon summoning storms with its breath involves the Chinese emperor Ch'in Shih Huang Ti—the same emperor responsible for building China's Great Wall. According to Chinese lore, dragons are intelligent and able to converse with humankind. Because he had wanted to converse with a dragon, Emperor Ch'in Shih Huang Ti requested an official visit with one of the rulers of dragonkind, called the dragon kings. The emperor's request was granted but under a single condition: The dragon king ordered that no person should attempt to draw a portrait of it as this particular dragon king thought himself to be quite ugly. The Chinese emperor agreed to this condition. However, during the meeting, one of the emperor's aides failed to abide by the dragon's request. Retelling the legend, author Peter Lum says,

> Unfortunately one of the emperor's men was so fascinated by the hideousness of the dragon king, the scales, the huge popping eyes, the whiskers, and the horns that protruded like forks of lightning even through the official headdress he was wearing, that he could not resist the temptation and started to sketch [the dragon] by using his foot and drawing an outline on the sand.[3]

Angered by this breach of trust on the part of Ch'in Shih Huang Ti's aide, the dragon with his mighty breath caused an awful storm to appear. All of Ch'in Shih Huang Ti's men were killed and the emperor himself barely escaped with his life. For a week afterward the storm raged, consequently destroying houses and crops, and taking the lives of many innocent people.

The Ability to Change Forms

In addition to the power of the dragon's breath, another consistent characteristic of all dragons in both Eastern and Western cultures is the creature's ability to change rapidly in size—although here, too, there are some key differences. The Western dragon is said to change in size as a part of its growth cycle; in other words, the infant dragon is typically described as small, wormlike, and seemingly harmless beast that develops rapidly into its ravaging adult form. Likewise, the Eastern dragon can also appear to be very small, but this is not necessarily the product of the Eastern dragon's growth; instead, the change in size and form is often a deliberate choice of the mature dragon.

Unlike popular fiction and films, which usually depict baby dragons as hatchlings from gigantic eggs, many early descriptions of the infant dragon of the Western variety are of a small wormlike creature. One well-known account in European lore is that recounted by the historical figure Sir John Lambton of fifteenth-century England. According to historical ballads, Sir John Lambton was fishing on the banks of the River Wear, located in England's present-day County Durham, when he came into contact with an infant dragon. As writer John Boyle relates:

> Soon afterwards [Lambton] felt something tugging at his line, and, pulling it in, he found he had caught, not a fish, but a strange-looking worm. Filled with disgust, he tore it from the hook and flung it into a nearby well. A stranger, who happened to pass by, looked at the creature in the well. It was, he said, in appearance like a newt, only with nine holes on either side of its mouth.[4]

According to Boyle, at the time, no one realized that the strange-looking worm was actually a dragon. Soon after, however, the worm began to grow. As Boyle describes:

> The Worm soon emerged from the well, which was now too small to contain it. It used to spend the daytime coiled round a rock in the middle of a river and at night made its way to a neighboring hill and twined itself round its base; it grew so fast that it could soon encircle the hill three times. This hill, on the north side of the Wear, about a mile and a half from old Lambton Hall [the residence of the Lambton family], is still called Worm Hill. The Worm now began to terrorize the whole countryside, sucking the cow's milk, worrying the cattle, devouring the lambs and committing every kind of depredation on the peasantry.[5]

The infant dragon is typically described as a small, wormlike, and relatively harmless creature.

The result was a dragon that continued to terrorize the countryside of County Durham until Lord Lambton himself was pressed to attempt to slay the ever-growing beast.

Another such instance involved the historical figure Ardashír, the first king of the Sāsānians, the rulers of Persia, who lived during the third century A.D. According to the ancient Persian text, Shāh-nāma (*Book of Kings*), in a city south of Persia on the shores of the Persian Gulf lived a man named Haftavād, whose daughter ascended a nearby mountain and spent the entire day spinning cotton. As she took a break from her spinning to eat, she bit into an apple and found a harmless-looking worm. Being a gentle girl, she removed the worm and placed it in her spindle holder.

Soon, though, like the worm caught by Lord Lambton, the girl's worm began to grow rapidly. As Boyle states:

> The creature began to increase in size; the spindle-holder became too small for it, and the girl made a beautiful casket for it to nestle in. Her father Haftavād was now a man of wealth and influence: leagued [or allied] with the chief men in town he overthrew and slew the ruler and then leaving the town built a citadel on the mountainside. The Worm had by this time outgrown the casket and a pool was constructed for it inside the citadel and a custodian appointed to feed it each day with a potful of rice. Years passed by, and the Worm grew to the size of an elephant.[6]

Eventually, the dragon of Haftavād's daughter became so great in size that it threatened the very kingdom of Persia and, with it, the power and prestige of King Ardashīr. Like Sir Lambton would more than ten centuries later, King Ardashīr was forced to slay the dragon.

Similarities in the East

Those who have confronted the Eastern dragon in its wormlike form have also been fooled into thinking that the creature is incapable of posing a threat. However, instead of finding out their mistake by watching the dragon develop over time, those who have confronted the Eastern dragon are made instantly aware of their error as the dragon reverts to its most ferocious form instantaneously.

One of the more recent and often cited stories of the Eastern dragon's ability to change forms supposedly occurred near the end of the eighteenth century. Just west of the city of Peking, there is a pool of water called Hei-lung Tan, which means Black Dragon Pool. Next to the pool is a temple where the people of China can still pay tribute to the pool's infamous resident, the black dragon itself.

According to Chinese lore, two hundred years ago Chinese emperor Ch'in visited the pool to attempt to speak with the dragon. As Lum relates:

> The emperor, with all the splendor of his court, entered the temple and stood by the side of the pool. There he burned incense and made offerings, calling upon the dragon to come forth and show himself. At first there was no response, but suddenly the emperor glanced down and there in the pool, almost under his feet, was a tiny black dragon, perhaps six inches long.[7]

A visitor to the Black Dragon Pool in China rows a dragon-shaped boat. Legend tells of a shape-changing dragon that lives in the pond.

The emperor was not impressed with the tiny dragon: He laughed aloud and then callously compared the dragon's minuscule size to that of his goldfish. The dragon itself did not respond. Instead, it simply changed form, growing larger and larger until its vast size caused the sun to be hidden from view. Legend relates that in response the emperor fell on his knees and begged the dragon's forgiveness. The emperor then promised to pay tribute regularly to the dragon of Hei-lung Tan. Luckily for the emperor, the dragon appreciated Ch'in's response and assumed its previous size only to disappear into the depths of the pond.

The Dragon as Guardian

As demonstrated by both the dragons that humbled Emperor Ch'in and John Lambton, many dragons are said to live in or near water sources. However, these are not the only places in which dragons are rumored to reside. Other dragon lairs include faraway islands or deep underground or undersea caves or palaces. But despite these differences in residence, two aspects of the dragon's lair are nearly always true: The dragon makes its home in out-of-the-way locations, and the dragon's lair is nearly always associated with the creature's treasure. As Boyle explains:

> Dragons or serpents (the terms are interchangeable) stand guard not only over water but over treasure, either buried treasure in the literal sense, or in the words of [the ancient Latin writer] Eliade, "every symbol embodying the sacred or able to bestow power, life or omniscience [knowledge]."[8]

Thus the dragon is nearly always seen as a guardian of some resource or object that is of potential value to humankind.

Human Contact and Treasure

If the dragon comes into contact with humans, it is nearly always because a human journeys to the abode of the drag-

on to gain access to its treasure. Typically, a hero often has to journey over vast distances in order to arrive at the dragon's abode. Such was the case for the Greek hero Jason, who sailed for many months from his home in Greece until he arrived at the relatively far-off Mediterranean land of Colchis, where he confronted an ever-watchful dragon. Jason hoped to rob the dragon of its treasure, the Golden Fleece, a ram's skin of pure gold that the dragon guarded by commandment of the ancient Greek gods. Yet another hero who sought to benefit from the material wealth of the dragon was Beowulf. Beowulf died from the wounds sustained by his fight with the dragon, but the book's author describes the wealth of the dragon as "priceless jewels and gleaming gold that littered the floor, and the wonderful things hanging from the wall."[9]

The Greek hero Jason is depicted in this marble frontispiece. In his hand he holds the golden fleece he captured from a dragon.

Gold was not all the dragon guarded. Another hero, the medieval knight Dieudonné de Gozon of the Order of Saint John, supposedly sought to secure from a dragon a chapel or shrine in which Christian pilgrims could pray. Like Jason, Dieudonné de Gozon also journeyed via ship in order to confront the dragon—this time to Rhodes, an island in the eastern Mediterranean Sea.

Eastern Riches

Likewise, Eastern descriptions of the dragon's lair—palaces in the case of the dragon kings—also include vast displays of wealth. As Lum describes:

> The [Chinese] Dragon-Kings were fabulously rich, and . . . [the emperor] himself could not imagine what treasures lay in their undersea palaces. The few men who had seen these spoke of palaces of crystal upheld by jade pillars, of coral and pearls, of precious stones washed down from the mountains by the great rivers of the earth.[10]

Yet, the Eastern dragon was not thought to be a miser like its Western counterpart. Instead, it offered the greatest of its treasures to humans it deemed worthy of such riches. In exchange for assistance or obedience from humans, the Eastern dragons gave gifts of pearls, rare jade, or even knowledge. Indeed, Chinese custom still contends that dragons were responsible for giving the gift of writing (in the form of Chinese characters) to humankind.

Regardless of the type of treasure, all dragons—Western or Eastern—were thought to be guardians of some kind of riches. Some dragon specialists, historians who specialize in dragon lore, have noted that this connection may stem from the simplest of treasures, one that is necessary to human survival—water. For example, John Boyle theorizes that all dragon myths have their roots in the Indo-Iranian belief that the god Indra slew a great dragon to release the waters of the world for humankind. Part of the belief in the dragon, he argues, is that all peoples were aware of their need for water to survive, whether the water source be the rain and storms caused by the Eastern variety or the springs and lakes occupied by many of the Western variety. Thus, Boyle concludes, dragons could have been an explanation for the loss of water sources. This connection with the value of water could then translate into other valuable items—such as gold or knowledge—with the continuance of the myth. However, even Boyle recognizes that not all traditions could owe their dragon lore to the Indo-Iranian tradition as it is highly unlikely that all traditions could have been perpetuated by a singular cause; instead, most historians assume that the tradition of the dragon probably developed independently in several cultures.

The Magical Properties of the Dead Dragon

The last common aspect of the dragon is the magical virtues of its body parts. The head, the scales, the teeth, and even the blood of the dead dragon have been ascribed various magical attributes. Testimonies to these magiclike qualities exist in both Eastern and Western dragon lore.

One of the earliest testaments to the presumed magical qualities of the dragon's parts originated in China. According to Chinese legend, an emperor of the Hsia dynasty (2205 to 1766 B.C.) collected foam from the mouths of two dragons and secured it in a box. Fifteen centuries later, the box was opened by another emperor. The foam immediately overflowed the box and spread throughout the palace. Slowly the foam took the form of a new dragon, which in turn impregnated one of the emperor's wives. From then on, the emperor's descendants claimed to be the descendants of the dragon itself.

In Western lore, historians seeking to describe the variety of uses of the dead dragon's parts often turn to the Roman scholar and author Pliny, and his *Natural History*, an encyclopedia written in Latin. Within *Natural History*, Pliny catalogs a number of different applications for parts of the dead dragon. The dragon's head, he writes, when buried underneath a threshold of a house, will bring good luck. Of the dragon's eyes, an ointment can be made which will ward off nightmares or other nighttime visions. Further, Pliny said, the dragon's teeth and vertebrae, when ground up and consumed, make people more susceptible to being commanded by their superiors.

Even earlier than the Middle Ages, the ancient Greeks also ascribed magical qualities to the dragon's body parts. According to the earliest of Greek sources, including the second century B.C. writer Apollodorus, the Greek hero Hercules used the venomous blood of a dragon to poison his arrows—one of which he used to kill a centaur (half man, half horse). The Greek hero Jason also benefited from the magical qualities of the dragon during his quest for the Golden Fleece; Jason buried the teeth of a dragon, from which grew an army of men. According to the first century A.D. Roman writer Ovid,

> Then [Jason] took the serpent's [dragon's] teeth . . . and scattered them over the land . . . as they grew, the teeth that had been sown [planted] took on new forms. Just as a baby acquires human shape in its mother's womb, and has all its body parts perfectly formed inside her body, emerging into the light of day when it is complete, so there rose up from the soil, in teeming abundance, a crop of human bodies which had been perfected in the womb of the pregnant earth. More surprising still, they emerged brandishing weapons, produced at the same time as themselves.[11]

Other magical qualities of the dragon can be located in the Norse legends, which originated in the far north of Europe with the Vikings. The Norse also speak of the virtues

of the dragon's blood although, unlike the blood used by Hercules, this blood was not considered poisonous. Instead, Norse legend stipulates that the blood of the dragon provides the drinker with hidden knowledge that surfaces only after the blood has been drunk. The Norse hero Sigurd learns this after slaying the monstrous dragon Fafnir. When Sigurd drinks Fafnir's blood, he is instantly aware of all of the languages of all animals, for he has quite literally digested that which the dragon knew when it was alive. Furthermore, when Sigurd bathed in the blood, he became nearly invincible to attack, much like the dragon itself.

In this classical sculpture, Hercules renders a fatal blow to the centaur poisoned by an arrow dipped in the blood of a dragon.

A carving on a church portal in Norway shows the Norse hero Sigurd killing the dragon Fafnir.

Although many of these magical qualities vary based on the culture of origin, what is important to historians and dragon specialists is that so many different cultures assign magical properties to the dead dragon. This is one more example of how all cultures that have expressed a belief in the dragon share a number of basic premises about this most elusive of beasts.

So Many Similarities

Although almost all historians are reluctant to admit the existence of dragons, there is little doubt that peoples of previous cultures believed dragons actually flew through the skies, breathed fire or rain, collected treasures, and engaged with humankind. Of further significance is that while each culture views dragons differently, so many similarities exist between so many separate cultures that it is tempting to speculate that some form of the dragon must have existed to account for these similarities.

Chapter 2

To Slay a Dragon

One of the most dominant characteristics of the Western dragon is that it is typically characterized as an evil beast that preys on humankind. The dragon is often a destroyer of crops. It routinely feeds on cattle, horses, and unsuspecting humans. In the worst scenarios, the dragon has been depicted as extorting human sacrifice—typically a young virgin girl—from townspeople who would otherwise all be totally slaughtered by the ravaging beast. As the people suffered, the dragon rested atop its fabled treasure, secure in its near invincibility. The only humans who dared challenge the dragon were the dragon slayers.

Most of the dragon slayers were the product of myth or fantasy. Yet that has not always been the case. Throughout history, people did believe in the existence of real dragons. Furthermore, even though a number of the more famous dragon slayers were probably fabricated, many historical figures were presumed to subdue or even kill a dragon using a variety of techniques and weaponry.

Belief in Dragons

Of primary importance to the advent of the Western dragon slayer is that the inhabitants of Europe and the Near East (although not typically considered Western, the people of the Near East subscribed to the Western idea of the dragon) truly believed in the existence of ninety-foot fire-breathing flying lizards. Proof of this belief exists both in their literature and in texts considered to be factually accurate and written at various times in history. Thus, although many of the tales of dragon slayers are obviously fictitious, the images of the dragon within these texts seem to be confirmed by other accounts, which were regarded as true when they were written.

Nowhere was this relationship between fiction and nonfiction closer than in medieval Europe during the twelfth and thirteenth centuries. During this time, the image of the knight in shining armor combating the dragon was substantially developed by French-speaking writers who sought to entertain the ruling royalty. These writers' favorite subjects were the knights of the legendary King Arthur, who presumably ruled the isle of Britain during the sixth century. Writers invented episodes in which many of King Arthur's knights confronted hostile dragons.

One of the better known of these fictional accounts involved a knight, Sir Guy of Warwick. The following English adaptation by A. R. Hope Moncrieff of the original Middle French texts describes in detail what Guy of Warwick saw as he rode horseback to confront a fearsome dragon:

> A grisly, gruesome beast it was, all covered, as in armor, with horrid black scales; it had claws like a lion and wings like an eagle; its eyes shone fiery red, and smoke belched forth from its mouth, when, on approach of the knight and his attendants, it gave a roar that echoed for miles around, and lashed with its huge tail till the ground shook as in an earthquake.[12]

During this same period, other types of descriptions of the dragon also existed, including the bestiary, medieval historical documents that indexed different types of beasts believed to have existed throughout the world (although most people today discount many of its entries as fiction). In one surviving untitled bestiary, a description of a dragon called Draco is surprisingly similar to the beast confronted by Guy of Warwick. Translator T. H. White writes:

> Draco the Dragon is the biggest of all serpents, in fact of all things on earth. The Greeks called it "draconta" and hence it has been turned into Latin under the name "draco."

King Arthur and his knights fend off a dragon in this fourteenth-century French manuscript.

When this dragon has come out of its cave, it is often carried into the sky, and the air near it becomes ardent [heated]. It has a crest, a small mouth and a narrow gullet [throat] through which it draws its breath or puts out its tongue.[13]

Because the descriptions of the dragon in both the adventures of Guy of Warwick and the bestiary are similar, it is possible that writers who incorporated dragons into their fictive accounts were not simply inventing the idea of the dragon. It is possible that some early writers were turning to catalogs like the bestiaries to provide material for their own fictive accounts. In other words, because the audiences of the Middle Ages may have believed in the existence of dragons, it is possible that the dragons were added to the stories of knights such as Guy of Warwick to make the heroic quests of the knights seem more believable. As a result, because people believed in the existence of dragons, they also believed it was necessary to kill them, for the Western dragon was seen not only as monstrous in its appearance, but also quick-tempered and evil with a special hatred for humankind.

The Evil That Dragons Do

Such beliefs were a result of humans' concern about the evil acts the dragon apparently committed. Although there are a number of different crimes attributed to the dragon, each crime led to only one option: Until a hero appeared on the scene to slay the beast, the people who lived near the dragon had no option but to give in to whatever it desired. In most cases, bowing to the will of a dragon meant either that the people had to live with the fear that the dragon might at anytime prey on their animals or the local human inhabitants, or that the local residents would have to sacrifice one of their own—typically on a regular basis—in order to satiate the hunger and wicked temper of the dragon.

One dragon who reportedly terrorized an entire populace was Malpasso, who lived on the Island of Rhodes. According to the official documents of the Order of Saint John (a militant religious order), whenever the creature needed to feed, it would devour inhabitants or pilgrims who sought to pray at a Christian shrine located on the island. As Moncrieff describes:

> [The dragon issued] forth morning and evening out of a dark cave in the side of the mountain, it not only made havoc among cattle and horses but often devoured the luckless country people and pilgrims on their way to the shrine, who were unable to fly for terror at the very sight of its dreadful fangs, or fell senseless to the ground over-powered by the venom of its fiery breath.[14]

Other examples of marauding dragons also exist in Western literature. For instance, the dragon confronted by Guy of Warwick had terrorized a kingdom in northern France for years. In his *Natural History*, Pliny reported that marauding dragons capable of slaying an elephant roamed the countryside in India eager to catch anyone unfortunate enough to be in their way. Even Beowulf's last battle against the great dragon was a result of the dragon's rampages across the countryside as it burned and killed everything in its path.

Human Sacrifice

Another common motif in dragon lore is the dragon demanding a sacrifice of the local inhabitants. Almost inevitably the final sacrifice is a beautiful young virgin, typically of royal blood. This act prompts the dragon slayer to arrive on the scene to save her. As Boyle relates:

> The story varies in details but as commonly told it runs thus. A certain country is infested by . . . a dragon . . . which would destroy the whole people if

a human victim, generally a virgin, were not delivered up to him periodically. Many victims have perished, and at last it has fallen to the lot of the king's daughter to be sacrificed.[15]

Although it was certainly an emotionally difficult chore, the sacrifice was always better than the alternative, which would have been complete devastation of the populace by the ravaging and unappeased dragon.

One account of a sacrificial maiden involves the renowned Greek hero Perseus, who sought to save the lovely Andromeda from the ravages of a great dragon who lived in the sea. According to the legend, Andromeda was chained to a rock to await the coming of the sea dragon sent by Poseidon, the Greek god of the ocean, whom Andromeda's mother had inadvertently offended. Renowned mythologian Thomas Bulfinch describes Andromeda as Perseus found her: "As Perseus looked down from his aerial height he beheld the virgin chained to the rock, and waiting the approach of the serpent. She was so pale and motionless that if it had not been for her tears and her hair that moved in the breeze, he would have taken her for a marble statue."[16]

Perseus, like many dragon slayers, was induced to try and slay the dragon because he fell in love with Andromeda's beauty. Other dragon slayers, however, are motivated out of kindness, religion, or even the desire for the prestige and glory that killing a dragon could bring.

How to Slay a Dragon

However, killing a dragon was no easy task. Dragons were typically viewed as nearly invincible because of their overwhelming size, breath weapon, and natural defense: metallic-like scales covering their bodies from nose to tail. Yet, the task was not an impossible one. Nearly all dragons were depicted as possessing some sort of weak spot, typically a place on their bodies that was unprotected by its scales. The dragon slayer's only hope for surviving an encounter with a dragon was to locate this weakness and use it to his advantage.

Perseus rescues the chained Andromeda from the awful sea dragon in this sixteenth-century painting.

Perseus's triumph over the great water dragon follows this recurrent pattern for slaying the great beasts: He, like many other dragon slayers, finds the dragon's weak spot where it is not protected by its scaly armor. As Bulfinch relates: "Wherever [Perseus] found a passage for his sword between the scales, he makes a wound, piercing now the side, now the flank as it slopes towards the tail. . . . Alighting on a rock which rose above the waves, and holding on by a projecting fragment, as the monster floated near he gave him his death stroke."[17]

Like Perseus, Beowulf needed to find his dragon's weak spot in order to kill it. Beowulf would have failed to slay his dragon had not his kinsman, Wiglaf, rushed to his aid as Beowulf unwisely and ineffectively continued to beat the dragon's scaly head with his sword; Wiglaf, on the other hand, avoided the head by striking the creature in a spot lower on its body, a technique that the maimed Beowulf copies, effectively dispatching the dragon. According to the author, "[Beowulf] pulled out a razor-sharp dagger . . . and ripped open the belly of the Worm."[18]

Likewise, Sir Guy of Warwick located the vulnerable spot of the dragon in the heat of battle only after failing to penetrate the creature's impervious scales. As Moncrieff describes:

> Deftly [Guy of Warwick] drew his sword, and struck mighty blows like a storm of hail. But the good blade ever glanced off these foul scales; nowhere could he find a spot at which to pierce the snaky folds. He was overthrown; the dragon coiled its vast length about his body, crushing his armor and holding him fast in a deadly grip.
>
> The watching squires raised a cry and gave their master up for lost. The knight himself had hardly hoped to save his life, yet, gathering all his strength

for one last blow, he thrust the sword down the monster's open jaws. At once, he felt its grasp loosened, so that he could again draw breath. Wrenching himself free . . . he pierced its body beneath the wings, where the scales did not cover it, and drove his sword up to the hilt. With a shriek, the dragon dropped to the ground, drenched by its black blood.[19]

Although there is no evidence to support the existence of Perseus, Beowulf, or Guy of Warwick, historians have noted that each of these heroes, as well as many others, all must resort to the same technique if they are to triumph in their lone battles against the dragon. As Jonathon Evans explains, examples like these use "the tradition that dragons, while generally impervious to weaponry, have a soft spot below the belly, under the wing, or elsewhere."[20]

Such traditions and similarities lead some researchers to wonder, then, if it were possible that dragons did exist and that the technique for killing them was known enough to have been included in the stories. Others contend, however, that the storytellers simply copied each other thereby creating the similarities. These coincidences would be easier to resolve if all the dragon slayers were simply fictive characters in a story. However, the mystery of the dragon deepens; not all dragon slayers were necessarily products of fantasy.

Dieudonné and Malpasso

Many accounts exist of actual heroes who claimed, or who were claimed by others, to have confronted the might of the dragon. Some of the most important are those dragon slayers who purportedly met the beasts alone using, like the fictive dragon slayers, the technique of locating the vulnerable weak spot of the dragon they were fighting. Some researchers suggest that these dragon-slaying episodes may

The dragon slayer Siegfried drives his sword into the soft spot of the dragon.

lend credibility to the myths surrounding the image of the dragon, therefore proving the existence of the dragon itself.

Dieudonné's presumed historical slaying of the great Rhodes dragon, Malpasso, is one such instance. Dieudonné de Gozon was known to be the third Grand Master (leader) of the Knights of Saint John in the fourteenth century (1346–1353). The beast he confronted was called

Malpasso, a dragon who lived on the Island of Rhodes in present-day Greece. Although the records that relate the confrontation between Dieudonné and Malpasso were said to be historically accurate by the Order of Saint John, the records that report the event were first composed two hundred years after the fact by a German pilgrim. And, the best known version was composed seventy years after that by Giacomo Bosio, an official historian of the Order of Saint John. Therefore, many scholars have suggested that the records were invented after the fact.

A modern-day man is dressed as a historic dragon-slaying Knight of the Order of St. John.

Yet, according to Bosio's account, Dieudonné de Gozon had witnessed the terrors and atrocities of Malpasso since his youth. He had also watched, along with the other Knights of Saint John, as knight after knight journeyed to the island in an effort to slay the dragon only to die trying. Dieudonné wanted to journey to the island himself, but he was not allowed because the first Grand Master forbid all the other knights from any further attempts; the Grand Master thought Malpasso to be invincible to all attacks.

However, Dieudonné was not to be thwarted. Instead, he carefully planned his attack in secret, plotting to take advantage of the dragon's only known weakness, its unprotected underbelly. As Moncrieff describes:

[Dieudonné] found out a cunning artificer [carpenter], and employed him to make a wooden figure which should exactly resemble the dragon in size, shape and color. Then he procured two bull dogs of the best breed, which he carefully trained to throw themselves upon this figure and hold it fast with their obstinate fangs, while he exercised his horse in riding boldly up to it; and when, by a mechanical contrivance [machine], [the wooden dragon] was made to rear in the air, he aimed his lance with firm eye at the belly, the only part of its body unprotected by scales.[21]

Once Dieudonné had perfected his and his animals' techniques, he journeyed to the Island of Rhodes to confront Malpasso. However, all did not go as planned. On seeing the actual dragon, Dieudonné's horse threw him to the ground and bolted. The result would have been fatal had it not been for the loyalty of his dogs. Moncrieff says:

The faithful dogs had not so ill learned their lesson. Now they fell upon the dragon, seized it with their fangs from beneath, and all its furious struggles and horrible cries could not force them to lose their hold. The monster, maddened with pain, reared its huge body in the air at the same moment [Dieudonné] recovered himself and rose to his feet. With all his might he drove his sword to the hilt in its white belly, unprotected by scales such as covered his back.[22]

Dieudonné returned to the castle belonging to the Order of Saint John as a hero. Years later, he was made the third Grand Master, and the records of the Order of Saint John say that his bravery and selflessness in the matter of Malpasso played a role.

Other Historic Slayers

The feats of dragon slaying was also attributed to a number of other historic persons throughout Western history. Furthermore, like Dieudonné de Gozon, each of these dragon slayers engaged in careful planning to take advantage of the dragon's weaknesses. Although, how these plans manifested themselves is often strikingly different.

One such historic individual was John Lambton, a fifteenth-century historical figure who, like Dieudonné de Gozon, is on record as being a knight of the Order of Saint John. Further, Lambton is the direct ancestor of the earls of Durham, which includes the present-day Lord Lambton of England. Although John Lambton's techniques for killing the dragon were quite different from Dieudonné's, they also took advantage of the creature's unprotected underbelly.

John Lambton was the catcher of the Lambton worm that, over time, grew into a full-fledged dragon that ravaged the English countryside. To slay that dragon, John Lambton had dozens of spear points attached to his armor. Then, sword in hand, he waited for the dragon on a rock it frequented in the middle of a river. The dragon and Lambton struggled until, as Lambton expected, the dragon wrapped itself like a snake around Lambton's body in an effort to crush him. The tighter the dragon squeezed, the more the beast injured itself on the spear points. Finally, weakened by its numerous wounds and the loss of blood, the dragon tried to withdraw, allowing Lambton the opportunity to finish the job with his sword.

Another historical dragon slayer was the Persian king Ardashir, who lived during the third century. Like Lambton, Ardashir also resorted to trickery, yet his was of a very different kind. Instead of trying to fight the dragon, Ardashir slipped it molten metal in lieu of food, thereby taking advantage of another of the dragon's weaknesses—

Ardashír (right), the third-century Persian king who used trickery to kill a dragon, receives his title as king.

its insatiable appetite. As the Shāh-nāma (*Book of Kings*) relates, moments after swallowing the molten metal, the dragon exploded into two pieces.

Other famous dragon slayers have been religious figures. Saint George, for example, reputedly saved a king's daughter from being sacrificed to a dragon. Similarly, the Middle Eastern saint El Khudr also slew a dragon to save a virgin from sacrifice; El Khudr had been made immune from the dragon's attack because of his faith in God.

Not all historical figures needed to slay the dragon to conquer it. Saint Simeon, for instance, reportedly healed a dragon; thereafter, says one author, "the creature coiled itself up and stayed quiet in one place, whilst all the people went by."[23] And Saint Martha is said to have tamed a dragon through her Christian faith so that it followed her back to the village where she allowed others to kill it with sticks and stones.

Saint Simeon, immortalized in a sixteenth-century church icon, healed a dragon rather than slay it.

Alexander the Great

Perhaps the most famous of all dragon slayers is also one of the most famous people in history, Alexander the Great, who lived from 356 to 323 B.C. Alexander was the king of Macedonia and one of the world's greatest conquerors. As a result of his conquests, his empire stretched throughout Europe, the Near East, and Asia. In a letter written by Alexander to his tutor, the philosopher Aristotle, Alexander the Great claims to have slain a dragon. Of great interest to dragon specialists is that Alexander is the only dragon slayer to have narrated his exploits in his own words. He therefore provides a firsthand account of the terrible nature of the dragon as well as the effort and planning required to slay it.

Alexander the Great leads a charge against fearsome dragons and other strange beasts in this thirteenth-century manuscript page.

In the letter Alexander describes how he led his army east from an area known as Prasiake, located in modern-

An ancient Greek coin shows the face of Alexander the Great who wrote personal accounts of his dragon-slaying adventures.

day India. As they prepared to ascend a mountain pass, the local inhabitants warned the king and his troops that they were in danger from a dragon that attacked all who scaled the mountain. The local inhabitants also revealed that they provided two oxen for the dragon daily in an effort to curb its mighty appetite.

Wanting to see the dragon for himself, Alexander accompanied the locals to the place where they left the oxen. As Alexander writes:

> I took some of the people of the land [with me], and set out from thence, and came to the bank of the river. And I commanded them to place the oxen as they were accustomed to do, and I and my troops stood upon the top of the mountain. And we saw

45

when the beast came forth from its den and came to the bank of the river. When I saw the beast, I thought that it was a black cloud which was standing upon the bank of the river, and the smoke which went forth from its mouth was like unto the thick darkness which comes in a fog. And we saw it crossing the river, and when as yet it had not reached the oxen, it sucked them into its mouth by the drawing in of its breath, as [if cast] by a sling, and swallowed them.[24]

Awed by the gigantic and monstrous nature of the dragon, Alexander realized that neither he nor his army could do direct battle with the beast and hope to win. Instead, the king concocted a plan that would play on the dragon's only weakness that Alexander could perceive—its appetite. As he relates:

Then I straightaway gave orders to bring two oxen of huge bulk, and to kill them, and to strip off their hides, and to take away their flesh, and to fill their skins with gypsum and pitch and lead and sulfur, and to place them on that spot. When they had done this, the beast according to its wont crossed the river again, and when it came to them, it suddenly drew both of the skins into its mouth and swallowed them. As soon as the gypsum entered its belly, we saw that its head fell upon the ground, and it opened its mouth, and uprooted a number of trees with its tail. And when I saw that it had fallen down, I ordered a smith's bellows [device used to pump air in order to increase a fire's temperature] and balls of brass to be heated in the fire and to be thrown into the beast's mouth; and when they had thrown five balls into its mouth, the beast shut its mouth, and died.[25]

Real or False Testimonies?

If accounts like those of Alexander or testimonies of the slaying of the Rhodes dragon are indeed factual, then dragons were apparently in conflict with some of the greatest heroes in history. However, respected scholars and historians have made numerous challenges to the authenticity of these dragon-slaying episodes.

Most skeptics begin by pointing out that the majority of these accounts of historical dragon slayers were recorded by other parties, often well after the fact. Skeptics believe that the story of the dragon was fabricated using the historical person as a factual point of reference to make the person sound even more legendary. As Boyle explains, the dragon-slaying myth can be accounted for "by the theory that popular memory, disregarding a man's real exploits, equips him with a mythical biography in which a battle with a . . . dragon plays an inevitable part."[26]

For example, skeptics have pointed out that the story of Dieudonné and Malpasso was written two hundred years after the actual event was presumed to have taken place. Further, they argue that the Order of Saint John had political reasons for inventing Dieudonné's triumph. Since the Knights of Saint John had recently been expelled from the area of Rhodes by the Ottoman Turks who controlled the area, they wanted to justify a comeback by citing their own valor and therefore value to the region. Critics conclude that later historians invented Malpasso. Similarly, Alexander the Great could have fabricated his own dragon-slaying episode to increase his own fame—something not unheard of for a conqueror who needed to maintain his prestige to retain power over a vast empire.

Chapter 3

The Wise Dragons of the East

Unlike the evil acts attributed to the Western dragon, the dragon of the East is most often characterized as a generous, benevolent creature whose key role is to act as a mediator between heaven and humankind. Eastern dragons are also seen as closely connected to the element of water—indeed, all natural events involving rain or storms are seen to be associated with the wiles of the dragon. This dual role, that of a kind creature associated with water, is cited in Eastern legends and historical documents, both of which testify not only to sightings of the dragon but also to intimate dragon-human relationships including certain peoples thought to have been relatives of the dragon itself.

Differences in Appearance

In overall appearance, the Eastern dragon, like its Western counterpart, is generally snakelike. However, despite these physical similarities, many specifics of the Eastern dragon's appearance differ sharply. These differences are what allow dragon specialists to identify the Eastern dragon. And perhaps more important, they contribute to the very different character of the dragon of the East.

The Chinese explain the appearance of the Eastern dragon as a collection of "resemblances," meaning the

In Eastern culture, dragons are closely connected with the element of water.

dragon can be described in comparison to other animals which it, in part, resembles. As the ancient Chinese philosopher of the Han dynasty (circa A.D. 1–400), Wang Fu, who believed in the existence of dragons, writes: "[A dragon's] horns resemble those of a stag, his head that of a camel, his eyes those of a demon, his neck that of a snake, his belly that of a clam, his scales those of a carp, his claws those of an eagle, his soles [of his feet] those of a tiger."[27] Resemblances like these have prompted a number of ancient Eastern scholars to comment on the origin of the dragon with respect to other animals of the earth. The most prominent was the belief that all animals possessed a kinship with the dragon and looked to it as their master. Others went so far to suggest that all animals were in fact descended from the dragon. What is telling is that the appearance of the dragon contributed to how it related to the world in which it was presumed to have lived.

Another revealing aspect of the dragon's description is its inheritance of the magiclike ability to fly as a result of its physical features. Even though the Eastern dragon might have wings like its Western counterpart, the wings are often depicted as small and do not contribute to the dragon's ability to fly. Instead, the Eastern dragon's ability to take to the air is attributed to a small swelling, or bump, located on the top of its head. According to Wang Fu: "Upon [the dragon's] head he has a thing like a broad eminence [a big lump] called *ch'ih muh*. If a dragon has no *ch'ih muh*, he cannot ascend to the sky."[28]

The scales of the adult Eastern dragon also contribute to its unique qualities. The mature dragon is said to have exactly 117 scales on its body, 36 of which are imbued with yin (passive forces) and 81 with yang (aggressive forces). The combination of both yin and yang is said to contribute to the balancing of the dragon's personality; in other words, as a result of its physical characteristics, the dragon is an

The Eastern dragon's ability to fly is associated with a prominent swelling, or bump, located on the top of its head.

aggressive creature, but it is able to control these aggressive tendencies through its more passive, or yin, physical components. The dragon is therefore not evil, though it is thought to be willful and has the capability of being ruthless if provoked.

Yet another specific feature of the Eastern dragon is the changing number of toes on each foot. In fact, it is possible to determine whether a dragon is of Chinese, Korean, or Japanese origin by the number of toes. Dragons of Japan, for instance, reportedly possess three toes, while the Korean dragon has four. All Chinese dragons until 206 B.C. possessed five toes. After that date, the Chinese emperor Kao Tsu decreed that only the "imperial dragon"—the image of the dragon king and the private emblem of the Chinese emperor himself—could possess five toes; all others would possess four. (Anyone who violated this rule was immediately sentenced to death.) As a result, Eastern peoples believed that migrating dragons would gain or lose toes depending on the region to which they moved.

Dragon Sightings and Bad Weather

Like its Western counterpart, there is no definitive evidence such as a discovery of archaeological evidence that proves Eastern dragons existed. However, even though physical evidence is lacking, believers in the dragon have pointed to other evidence that they believe proves the creature's existence—notably, recorded dragon sightings. Within the numerous written histories and lore of the East, there are many documented examples of people claiming to have seen the Eastern dragon. And because the Eastern dragon was seen as a producer of storms through the power of its breath, nearly all of these sightings were accompanied by radical, and often catastrophic, changes in weather.

One testament to the existence of the Eastern dragon comes from an official Chinese historical document, *History of the Sung Dynasty*. According to the manuscript, in the year A.D. 973, a dragon rose from a well and started severe rains that destroyed houses, uprooted trees, and caused floods that killed inhabitants of the area. The next year, the tower of a nearby castle was struck by lightning;

again the dragon was involved. The manuscript describes the incident as follows:

> In Ti cheu [an ancient city in central China] there fell a fire from the air [lightning] upon the tower of the Northern gate of the castle. There was a creature which embraced the eastern pillar. It had the shape of a dragon and a golden color . . . and its breath smelled very bad. In the morning, when people looked for it, there were on the upper part of the wall thirty-six smoke stains, the traces of claws.[29]

Other sightings of the dragon are also noted in ancient Chinese records. The manuscript *Kiang-Si t'ung-chi* claims

A Chinese tile panel reveals a dragon with five toes on each foot.

that in the year A.D. 1156 a particularly furious thunder-storm raged in the area of inner China. Darkness descend-ed on the country for more than a month. Furthermore, during the storm, residents heard a constant roarlike cry all night and day. The manuscript explains that this was the roar of a well-known dragon, one that had caused the storm as it bellowed from a neighboring pond. Another sighting, appearing in a manuscript called *Fei such luh*, reports that passersby in a small village witnessed a small dragon the size of a snake creeping out from a crack of an unplastered house. Once the dragon had fully emerged, it grew in size before the amazed eyes of witnesses. The dragon then flew into the sky; immediately the sky turned dark with clouds and the people had to take shelter from a horrific storm.

Interestingly, although these storms were often cited as causes of misery and even death for humankind, the dragon itself was never regarded as evil. Instead, the storms were looked at by Eastern peoples as both good and bad. Similar to the opposing forces of yin and yang within the physical makeup of the dragon, the role of the dragon as a rain giver meant that the storms that caused so much grief also sup-plied water. In other words, humans had to accept the hor-rors of the storms if they were to reap its life-providing benefits.

The Dragon Kings

The benefits offered to humanity by the Eastern dragon were not limited only to the provision of water. The most important of these other benefits were typically doled out to humankind by the presumed rulers of dragon kind, the dragon kings. The number of dragons said to exist within the East is near infinite: They inhabit every storm and every pool of water; they exist within the ocean and also within the waves that mar the coastline; even the wind is the

product of a dragon's breath. Yet all dragons were said to respect a closely tied political system that was governed by the relatively few dragon kings. As Lum explains:

A dragon hides from prehistoric man inside storm clouds. Eastern cultures associated storms with dragons.

The dragons are indeed so numerous that they are thought to have set up government departments which look after the administration of the dragon kingdom. . . . The *Shui Fu*, or Treasury of the Waters, governs the entire dragon world, but this ministry in turn has many subdivisions. Among them is the Supreme Council and the Body of Dragon Ministers, the Ministry of Salt Waters, which includes both the General Department of Salt Waters and the Special Department of Salt Waters, and the Department of Sweet Waters.[30]

The dragon kings lived in great palaces, all of which were located underwater. The location of one palace is described in the ninth-century Chinese manuscript *Luh i ki*. Author M. W. De Visser summarizes:

[The palace] was situated under a small island about five or six days navigating from Su-chen (in Kiang-su province). Even when there was no wind, the waves were so high there that no vessel dared approach it directly. At every high tide, however, when the water overflowed the island and the high waves were not to be seen, the ships could pass there. At night a red light was seen from afar above the water on this spot, bright like sunlight, which extended more than a hundred miles square and reached the sky.[31]

Other palaces were said to exist at the bottoms of lakes or deep rivers. The one common link was that they were typically inaccessible to humankind. There were exceptions though; a number of documents attest to humans being received into the palaces of the dragon kings.

Yet, even though a human might be granted an audience with a dragon king, the human would rarely see the dragon king in his natural shape. Instead, the dragon king would work its unique magic on himself, thereby taking the physical form of a human being. But even in the guise of a human, the dragon king was said to possess dragonlike features, including green skin and eyes, horns, scales, and sometimes even tails. (Indeed, the dragon king could take on any form he wished, and there are recorded stories of them in the guises of fish, dogs, cattle, and trees.)

Eastern Treasures

Many of these visitors to the palaces of the dragon kings were emperors or others of immense social stature, but humans of more humble beginnings also were received. Regardless of social stature, all visitors typically departed the palace in a better situation than when they arrived because the dragon kings were known to be quite generous with their treasures.

Like the Western dragons, Eastern dragons were known for the treasures they hoarded in their lairs. Yet unlike the Western miserly dragon, Eastern dragon kings could be generous—especially if humankind aided the dragon in some way. Sometimes the dragon king rewarded a human with something from his vast hoard of collected wealth, including gems, pearls, or jade. But the most prized gifts the dragon kings had to offer were none of these. The luckiest of visitors came away with much more.

One example of such a lucky visitor was Lui I, a student who more than four thousand years ago returned to his village after failing his annual school exams. While walking along the road, Lui I espied a young woman herding goats. He was immediately struck by the girl's beauty, but also by her apparent sadness. When he asked the girl if he could be of assistance, the girl responded that she was the daughter of the dragon king of Tung T'ing Lake. She had recently married the son of the dragon king of the river Ching, yet her new husband ignored her and forced her to work. At the request of the distraught princess, Lui I agreed to explain her difficulties to her father.

On receiving entrance to the lake, Lui I was immediately struck by the richness of the underwater palace, which included an abundance of jade, pearls, and gems. But none of the riches compared to the grandeur of the dragon king himself. The dragon king stood in the middle of his great hall. While guised in human form, he still retained a wide dragonlike mouth and a flowing green beard. In his hands he held a jade tablet. When Lui I explained the reason for his visit, the dragon king's brother, a red dragon, avenged the wicked treatment of his niece by killing her husband.

In reward for aiding the dragon king's daughter, Lui I received more than simply great wealth. According to Lum: "The kings of the sea held a great feast. And in the end, although he insisted he was not worthy, Liu I married the beautiful young dragon princess and was granted the power of being equally at home in water or on land. He was also granted a dragon's life, which is ten thousand years."[32]

Thus, through the gift of the dragon king's daughter as his wife, Liu I and all of his children were able to claim fame and wealth through their kinship with a dragon king.

The Gift of Knowledge

The most coveted gift that the dragon kings could offer was knowledge. The dragon kings were believed to possess great wisdom. The most famous of these gifts of wisdom was said to be presented by a great yellow dragon king in China. And, although the gift was made to a single person, those who eventually benefited from it were all of the Eastern peoples.

According to Chinese lore, in 2875 B.C., as Emperor Fu Hsi crossed the Lo River in a small boat, he encountered a dragon. On the dragon's back were black spots in various designs. On arriving home, Fu Hsi immediately

drew these eight characters, which subsequently became the eight primary characters, or trigrams, of the *I Ching*, a method of reading and predicting fortunes that is still used today. Even more important, these trigrams formed the basis of the Chinese written characters, which are used still in China, Taiwan, and Japan.

A yellow dragon sculpture stands near the entrance of a temple in Thailand.

Because of this gift, the yellow dragon king is said to be the giver of writing, and therefore culture, to humankind. Further, representations of the yellow dragon king can be found in temples used for worship, and these images usually include the dragon carrying an astrological map or several books on its back in honor of its contribution. In fact, the gifts of wisdom attributed to the dragon kings, when combined with the other supernatural qualities of the dragon, led many to conclude that the Eastern dragon had a spiritual quality. Thus, these dragons have been thought to be spiritual forces, angels, or even gods.

The Status of the Dragon

The ancient Chinese philosopher Kwan Chung rationalized that the dragon must be a god, or *shen* in Chinese, because of its unique abilities. As he explains in his manuscript *Kwan tsz* (*The Philosopher Kwan*):

> A dragon in the water covers himself with five colors. . . . If he desires to become small, he assumes the shape resembling that of a silk worm, and if he desires to become big, he lies hidden in the world. If he desires to ascend, he strives towards the clouds, and if he desires to descend, he enters a deep well. He whose transformations are not limited by days, and whose ascending or descending are not limited by time, is called a god.[33]

Yet calling the Eastern dragon a *shen* did not mean that the dragon was not responsible to humanity or other gods. Instead, the Eastern dragon was regarded as a messenger between heaven and the earth. In this capacity, dragons have not only been portrayed as providers of water, but as defenders of humankind.

The dragon's ascension to heaven to communicate with the gods was attributed to all dragons of Eastern cultures. Indeed, the Eastern dragon was said to be able to leap to heaven in a single bound. A Japanese manuscript titled *Wakan sansui zue* and written in A.D. 1713, describes such an ascent.

According to the manuscript, an unnamed man witnessed a little dragon in the form of a snake swimming on the shores of Lake Biwa in Japan. The dragon swam to shore, climbed upon the water rushes, danced among the rushes, then returned to the surface of the water. It repeated these movements many times, and each time the dragon grew in size. Finally, the creature ascended into the sky, which suddenly became pitch black with clouds. A shower of rain commenced as the dragon entered the clouds; but, as soon as the dragon disappeared from view, the sky became blue once again. The unnamed author of the manuscript explains the dragon's initial behavior, saying, "The climbing upon the rushes and dancing about was probably a preparatory exercise for ascending to heaven."[34]

The dragon's ability to ascend to heaven is vital to its success at providing for and defending humankind. Although the dragon is regarded as the provider of water, even the dragon kings were thought to be subservient to the gods of heaven. Thus, in times of drought, the dragons would have to beg the gods of heaven to allow them to provide rain for humanity.

One of the oldest legends involving the connection between dragons and heaven demonstrates the legendary extremes to which a dragon was willing to go in its efforts to defend humanity from the wrath of heaven. According to this legend, initially no rivers existed in China. As people populated the country, they sought to grow crops, but the absence of water made this nearly impossible. Four dragons who lived in the Eastern Sea—the yellow dragon, the long dragon, the black dragon, and the pearl dragon—noticed the plight of mankind. They ascended to heaven to confer with the ruler of the gods, Yu-Huang-Shang-Ti, also known as the Jade Emperor, but he refused to allow rain to fall. The four dragons rebelled against the gods and caused it to rain because they had decided that the Jade Emperor's decision was cruel and unjust.

However, the Jade Emperor was not pleased with the rebellion of the four dragons. He therefore punished the dragons by imprisoning each beneath mountains in different corners of the country. Despite this punishment, the four dragons did not regret their gift. Indeed, each dragon turned himself into a river to escape the confines of the mountains and provide permanent water sources for humankind. Thus China's four primary rivers are said to have been formed. To this day, each bears one of the dragon's names: the Heilong (black dragon) River of the far north; the Huang (yellow dragon) River and the Chang (long dragon) River of central China; and the Zhu (pearl dragon) River of the south.

The Dragon and the Emperor

Because dragons were believed to have access to heaven, Eastern peoples often revered dragons as their angelic guardians. Yet, the rulers of the East—the emperors—were often said to be favored by the gods because of their lineage, which allowed them to create the laws of their territories. Many Eastern emperors were said to be in contact with heaven via exclusive relationships with the dragons themselves.

In Eastern mythology, the yellow dragon became the rich source of water that nourishes the fertile Yellow River Valley in China.

The emperors of the East were most certainly some of history's most privileged individuals. Their commands became the law of the land. They ruled from grand palaces where they were pampered by servants. Within these palaces were riches beyond the dreams of everyday citizens, even by today's standards. And perhaps most important, the emperors were said to have a liaison with heaven through their connections with the dragons. In fact, much of the historical evidence that attests to the possible existence of dragons in the East is in reference to the Eastern emperors themselves—they were reportedly seen within the company of dragons; indeed, some emperors were thought to be descended from dragon blood.

The symbolic dragon has represented the power of the emperors since the oldest recorded times in China. The earliest known reference appears in the manuscript *Shu King*, in which the Emperor Shun is said to have requested a viewing of his ancestor's clothing. In the words of the manuscript, Shun said, "I wish to see the emblematic figures of the ancients: the sun, the moon, the stars, the mountain, the dragon, and the variegated animals [pheasants]."[35] The emblematic figures, including the dragon, to which Emperor Shun refers, are embroidered on a robe presumably belonging to Shun's historical predecessor, Emperor Hwang Ti, said to have ruled in China as early as the twenty-seventh century B.C. Indeed, the use of the dragon symbol on an emperor's belongings appeared as late as the 1500s; all items associated with the Chinese emperors were named after the dragon. Thus, the emperor wore dragon robes, slept in a dragon bed, and even drank from a dragon cup.

Assisting the Emperors

Yet the dragon's association with the emperors of the East was more than symbolic. A number of recorded documents

A dragon figure, associated with Chinese royalty, stands out on this ancient cloisonne enamel cup.

claim that emperors conferred with or received aid from dragons. Such was the case with Emperor Hwang Ti, who was reported to have ridden into the sky on a dragon's back to confer with the gods of heaven. Hwang Ti was also said to have enlisted the aid of dragons in combat. Ancient Chinese records—the *Bamboo Annals*—report that Hwang Ti used a great dragon to attack troops belonging to a rebel challenging his authority. The rebel and his army were killed.

Other emperors of China were also said to have contact with dragons. Emperor Shun, for instance, was reportedly assured of his right to become emperor by a dragon sent by heaven. According to De Visser, "The Emperor Shun . . . was visited by a yellow dragon which came out of the river Loh. On its scaly armor the inscription: 'Shun shall ascend the Throne' was visible."[36]

Furthermore, dragons often aided emperors on a regular basis. As late as the eighth century A.D., Emperor Ming Hwang was said to have received a dragon's assistance. Returning from a victorious battle, the emperor attempted to cross a river by boat. A dragon reportedly appeared, and, in deference to the battle the emperor had just won, carried on its back the emperor's boat across the river. Emperor Ming was moved by the kindness and loyalty of the dragon, so he thanked it and gave it wine. Likewise, so that none should doubt his right to the Chinese throne, Emperor Yü was said to travel across his great empire via a carriage drawn by two dragons. According to Chinese ancestral records, entitled simply *Historical Records*, Emperor K'ung Kiah supposedly tamed two dragons and kept them in his service; as a result, he attained the family name of Yü lung, or "dragon ruler."

Emperor-Dragon Relationships

Yet perhaps none of these manuscripts suggests such a firm relationship between dragons and emperors as those that attest to an emperor who was in fact of dragon blood himself. Fu Hsi, China's first emperor, reportedly had a dragon's tail; his successor, Shen Nung, was fathered by a dragon; and Emperor Ta Yu took the shape of a dragon to oversee the distribution of water in his kingdom. Likewise, in Japan, the emperor was often said to be a dragon. Indeed, because the Japanese people believed that anyone who actually saw a dragon might die from fright, those who spoke with the ancient Japanese emperors addressed them through a bamboo screen designed to hide their dragonlike features.

As a result of these emperor-dragon relationships, the Eastern dragon was an integral part of the social structure of the peoples of the East. Instead of journeying great distances to locate dragons as the heroes of the West did, believers in the Eastern dragon had to look only to their own leaders and the world around them to locate the effects of this mysterious beast.

Descendants of the Dragon

Today, many scholars find these tales of dragons even more difficult to believe than their Western counterparts. The faith in dragons as elemental forces of water or as representatives of heaven no longer survives in the East. This disappearance of faith combined with the lack of physical proof, such as dragon bones or fossils, means that most people in the East think of the dragon as a mythic animal invented to explain natural occurrences like floods or droughts.

However, despite this disbelief, remnants of the dragon still exist within contemporary Eastern cultures. For instance, dragons are still used as everyday symbols. Their images adorn temples, palaces, walls, and bridges in China and Taiwan. In Japan, too, the image of the dragon can be found throughout the country, preserved on buildings that date back to ancient times. Indeed, the Chinese commonly refer to the dragon in everyday language. According to Lum:

> In some of the ancient books it is described how fish from all the seas and the rivers of the earth gather together at certain times below the Lung Men [Dragon Gate] falls and "those who can pass on upstream turn into dragons, while those who cannot bump their heads and bruise their cheeks." That is why in China the expression "The carp has leaped through the dragon gate" is used to describe success, especially in examinations, and why a fish leaping through a waterfall is such a favorite theme in Chinese and Japanese art.[37]

Furthermore, contemporary Chinese still call themselves *Lung Tik Chuan Ren*, or descendants of the dragon. In this way, the survival of the dragon myth is almost assured.

Chapter 4

Origins of the Dragon

Many questions remain regarding the reality of the dragon within both Eastern and Western cultures, but answers and explanations are elusive. Although it seems unlikely that fire-breathing monsters fought knights in medieval Europe, or that dragons were responsible for storms and acted as messengers of heaven in the East, dragon scholars have been unable to arrive at a single cohesive theory to explain how dragon lore could have evolved in so many regions of the world. They do have some theories, however.

Among scholars and historians, two major theories have emerged that explain how this spread of dragon lore could have occurred. One argues that the dragon was a product of a single culture, perhaps the ancient Egyptians, which then spread throughout the globe. The other argues that the dragon, as a mythical creature, owes its beginnings not to a single civilization but to the shared values of all primitive people as they tried to explain the natural world that surrounded them.

The Question of Egypt

Of those specialists in dragon lore, probably none has had more of an impact on current theory as the scholar Grafton Elliot Smith. In his book *The Evolution of the Dragon*, Smith traces the origin of the dragon concept to ancient Egypt. Interestingly, even though his discussion of Egyptian lore is the focus of his argument, Smith's theories on the dragon's origin do not involve the dragon at all. Instead, Smith focuses on the ancient Egyptian gods and how these gods may have *become* dragons only much later in history.

Ancient Egypt was a vast and highly developed culture. The existence of the pyramids and hieroglyphics (a form of picture writing) attest to that. Yet, like any culture, ancient Egypt took many years to developed. Indeed, archaeological findings have dated the beginnings of ancient Egypt as early as 3300 B.C.; the civilization did not reach its peak until nearly two thousand years later. During the earliest times, the religion of the ancient Egyptians developed as different areas of Egypt incorporated new local gods into their growing pantheons (collections of gods). Of these were Osiris, Isis, Seth, and Horus, who was, Smith argues, the most influential in building the dragon myth. The result was a very detailed saga in which the gods themselves struggled for power.

In Egyptian mythology, Osiris was the husband of Isis, both of whom were gods and leaders of the Egyptian people. Seth, the brother of Osiris, was jealous of Osiris's power and plotted his destruction. Seth trapped his brother, drowned him in the Nile, and then chopped his body into fourteen pieces. As an immortal, Osiris crossed over to the Egyptian land of the dead, where he took charge of the Egyptian afterlife. Osiris, though, no longer had any power over the living world, so Seth succeeded in stripping his brother of his kingdom. Yet, unbeknownst to Seth, Osiris and Isis had had a son, Horus. When Horus reached manhood, he sought to avenge the death of his father by confronting Seth and his allies in a series of battles.

As the battles between Horus and Seth's servants progressed, Horus took a unique form, one which Smith argues became the basis for the world's belief in dragons. During the battles, Horus assumed the form of the sun in

A sculpture from the seventh-century B.C. depicts the Egyptian god Horus with the head of a falcon.

which he possessed many dragonlike attributes, notably wings, the monstrous head of a falcon, and fire-spitting snakes that replaced an eye he had lost in an early conflict with Seth. As Smith describes:

> Horus assumed the form of the sun equipped with the wings of his own falcon and the fire-spitting . . . serpents. Flying down from heaven in this form he was at the same time the god and the god's weapon. As a fiery bolt from heaven, he slew [his] enemies . . . now identified with his own personal foes, the followers of [Seth].[38]

Furthermore, Horus took on another dragonlike association. His father, Osiris, came to be associated with water. Thus, Horus was as well. Smith explains: "Osiris also was the weapon of destruction, both in the form of the flood (for he was the personification of the river) and the rainstorms from heaven."[39]

As a result, Horus became a dragonlike god and was identified with fire while also wielding a considerable influence over the weather. He also possessed wings and the ability to fly. Because of these attributes, Horus embodies the principal abilities of both the Western and the Eastern dragons. Smith concludes that all dragon stories probably stem from contact with Egyptian culture, particularly the borrowing and exaggerating of certain traits. The Eastern dragon, he says, is a result of exaggerating the dragon's relationship with water. And the Western dragon is a result of early Greek mythology, which applied the image of the dragon to the enemy of the sun god, meaning that the dragon became a crueler and more sinister creature.

However, Smith's arguments have been critiqued as being too simple. Much of this criticism stems from Smith's assumption that Egyptian myths possess a unique place in the history of the world. As Evans argues:

"[Smith's theory] is a reasonable explanation, although it depends upon Smith's bias in favor of Egyptian cosmology as the fountainhead [origin] of world mythology."[40]

The First Dragon?

The first dragon probably came from the Sumerians, a renowned civilization in the Tigris-Euphrates River valley in Mesopotamia, now present-day Iraq. As early as 3000 B.C., the Sumerians had already established Uruk, the world's first city. Over time, the Sumerian culture gave way to the Babylonians; however, the two were in essence made up of the same people and shared similar mythology. Thus, the world's first dragon, called Tiamat by the Babylonians, has its roots in Labbu, a Sumerian monster that was depicted as a sea-dwelling snake and was associated with the creator of the universe.

Tiamat had a profound influence on the development of the Western dragon. In fact, all Western dragons would later be modeled on this wicked creature. As Arthur Cotterell describes her: "Tiamat was imagined to be a composite creature, part animal, part serpent, part bird, revolting in appearance, and dreadful in anger. She was evil: a she-dragon."[41] Although Tiamat was most definitely horrible, she was also associated with life-giving creation. She was simultaneously a goddess and mother of all the gods, and terrible, vengeful, and full of malice toward her own children. Indeed, she became so annoyed with her children's presence that she resolved to wage war on them, thereby destroying all she had created.

On learning of this plan, the rest of the gods were terrified. Finally, they decided to nominate someone to confront Tiamat and attempt to kill her. According to Cotterell:

When news of the fearsome preparations Tiamat was making for war reached the gods, there was

This doglike dragon made of glazed brick comes from the gates of Ishtar at Babylon. It symbolizes Marduk, champion of the gods who defeated Tiamat.

dismay and despair. Along with her second husband Kingu and an army of monstrous dragon and serpent forms, Tiamat, the mother of the gods, was bent on universal destruction. Chaos menaced the world. Then Anshar [Tiamat's son] proposed that Marduk [Tiamat's great-grandson] be appointed as the divine champion and armed "with matchless weapons" for the terrible battle. . . . With bow and trident, club and net, and an armory of winds, [Marduk] rode his chariot into the fray. When Tiamat opened her jaws to swallow him, he launched a raging wind straight into her mouth, so that she could not close it, shot an arrow into her belly, and slew her.[42]

The defeat of Tiamat by Marduk was significant to the way the Babylonians viewed the world. Tiamat was the realm of chaos, and she sought to destroy her children along with the world that they created, the world of humankind. Marduk was therefore the proponent of order and stability as he defended the world against the evil intents of Tiamat. As Cotterell explains, the myth of Tiamat represented "the chaos of original matter [Tiamat] constantly at odds with the created order [Marduk and humankind]."[43] The fact that Marduk triumphed meant that the world in which the Babylonians lived was secure.

Tiamat and the Western Dragon

Numerous scholars have hypothesized that this relationship between Tiamat and Marduk was the paradigm for the Western dragon's image and popularity. Although Tiamat was slain, the influence of her beastly appearance and evil intent was not. Through their contact with the early Greeks, the Babylonians passed on the image of Tiamat as well as the fight against chaos that she represented. Tiamat, and therefore the dragon itself, became the embodiment of malice and was incorporated into the developing mythology and literature of the Greeks.

This connection is most clearly seen in the Homeric Hymn to Apollo, a poem in which the god Apollo—who, like Horus, is affiliated with the sun—must slay a dragon that threatens to disrupt the building of the oracle at Delphi, a place from which Apollo communicated the order and divine will of the gods. In time, this portrait of the Western dragon reached across the European continent because of the popularity of literary tales like *Beowulf*, and also because of the conquests of empires—including the famed Macedonian Empire under Alexander the Great.

Biblical Dragons

The most effective text to spread the word of the dragon, however, was none other than the Bible. Many scholars surmise that because Tiamat was viewed as the representative of chaos, it matched perfectly with the Christian concept of the devil, or Satan, since he too, was seen as representing chaotic forces that were contrary to the ordered and heavenly vision of the Christian god. Because of this close relationship between chaos and order, third century B.C. translators of sections of the Bible made imagistic connections between Greek mythology, and therefore Tiamat, and the Hebrew portrayals of Satan. Satan is twice depicted as a great dragon in the Bible. In the final chapters of the Apocalypse, Saint John is said to see

> an angel coming down from heaven, holding in his hand a key to the bottomless pit [Hell] and a great chain. And he seized the dragon, that ancient serpent, who is the Devil and Satan, and bound him for a thousand years, and threw him into the pit, and shut it and sealed it over him, that he should deceive the nations no more. (20:1-3)

Additionally, eight chapters earlier, the devil is said to be "a great red dragon, with seven heads and ten horns, and seven diadems [crowns] upon his heads." (12:3)

Therefore, some argue, many of the saints and other dragon slayers with religious connections can be said to be slaying the devil. This would seem almost certainly the case with Saint George, the most well known of the saintly dragon slayers. According to legend, Saint George found a maiden by a lakeside. She informs him of a dragon that has devoured maidens in sacrificial tribute; this maiden will be next. George immediately draws the dragon into battle. After a heated confrontation, in which Saint George's lance is shattered, he finally slays the dragon with his sword.

Despite this story, there are no official records of Saint George slaying a dragon. Indeed, the dragon-slaying episode was added more than seven centuries after Saint George's probable lifetime. As Reverend F. G. Holweck

Saint George wields his sword against the dragon of the lake.

explains with respect to what scholars know of the fifth-century saint:

Though honored alike in the East and the West, Saint George is one of those saints about whom we know little. According to a legend, he was born of noble Christian parents in Cappadocia [in present-day Turkey]. As he grew to manhood he became a soldier; his courage in battle soon won him promotion, and he was attached to the personal staff of Emperor Diocletian [of the Roman Empire]. When this ruler decided to enter upon his campaign of persecution [against the Christians], Saint George resigned his commission and bitterly complained to the Emperor. He was immediately arrested and when promises [of wealth and power] failed to make him change his mind, he was tortured with great cruelty. . . . At last he was taken to the outskirts of the city and beheaded. . . . The episode of delivering the king's daughter from the power of a dragon cannot be traced further back than the 12th or 13th century.[44]

Many scholars assume, then, that Saint George's dragon-slaying episode was probably a metaphorical representation of his willingness to stand up to the non-Christian emperor, and ultimately the forces of Satan.

Still, much of this is conjecture. Although some scholars have sought to portray the development of the Western dragon as stemming from a single source, others have not been so sure. Indeed, this skepticism has led some scholars to conclude that the image of the dragon may have simply arisen independently among several if not all Western cultures. According to Evans:

It is probably best to avoid the temptation to search for the original dragon and to posit [suggest] the idea, as some scholars recently have done, that in the history of the dragon, "each culture responded to some similar need in their mythology to produce a dragon-like creature" and that the dragon itself has been invented again and again independently throughout the world.[45]

Legends of India and the East

The monstrous Tiamat was not the only dragon to have affected so vast an area and so many cultures. The region of India also contributed a great deal to the dragon's development, notably the Eastern dragon. As was the case in Babylonia, Indian mythology also based its belief in dragons on the struggle between two gods. In this case, the god is Vritra, the moon, whose ongoing battle with the sun god Indra is remarkably similar to the battles of the Egyptian gods, Horus and Seth. Of further significance, with the spread of Buddhism from India—its place of origin—to China, the Indian belief in the dragon influenced the unique development of the Eastern dragon, most specifically its benevolent attitude and its position as guardian of the waters.

In Indian mythology, the monstrous and immortal serpent Vritra controlled the waters of the world by holding them within its vast coils. In order to release the waters into the world, the sun god Indra slew the serpent. Yet this killing of Vritra was not viewed as a one-time event. As the myth developed, it was used to explain the phases of the moon, meaning the nightly changes in the visible shape of the moon. As John Hopkins explains in *Religions of India*:

> Old legends are varied [but] the victory over Vritra is now expounded [explained] thus: Indra, who slays Vritra, is the sun. Vritra is the moon who swims in the sun's mouth on the night of the new moon. The sun rises after swallowing him and the moon is invisible because he is swallowed. The sun vomits out the moon, and the latter is then seen in the west, and increases again, to serve the sun as food. In another passage it is said that when the moon is invisible he is hiding in plants and waters.[46]

Therefore, the two immortals, the dragon slayer Indra and the serpent itself, Vritra, played out their battle cyclically as the phases of the moon, their twenty-eight-day struggle presumably beginning and ending throughout eternity.

In fact, because Indra is seen as the swallower of the moon, scholars have pointed out that it takes on characteristics of a serpent. Thus, the Indian myth in its most

The Indian god Indra (center) is armed with sword and knife in this ancient wall painting at Ajanta Caves in India.

mature form depicts both Indra and Vritra as dragons, and the phases of the moon are their endless chase within the night sky. The dragon Indra seeks the release of the waters of the world while the dragon Vritra seeks to hold them from humankind.

India and the Dragon of the East

This connection between water and the phases of the moon is what has allowed scholars to trace the origins of the Eastern dragon to the mythological beliefs of India. In fact, the role of the dragon king as a protector of treasure and guardian of water sources almost certainly relates directly to the myths of India. Not only did people in the East become aware of Indian mythology, but they also adopted much of it since Buddhism incorporates the Indian myths by relying on dragon imagery. However, these connections do not account for the whole history of the Eastern dragon. Indian Buddhism undoubtedly affected the role and purpose of the Eastern dragon, but Buddhism did not arrive in China until after the image of the dragon was already a widely used symbol, which means that other influences must have existed.

In China, the dragon is often seen in connection with a pearl or silver ball. In fact, most images depict the ball alongside the dragon. The exact nature of this ball has been elusive; its meaning has changed over the centuries. The ball has represented the sun, the moon, the thunder, or even as a testament to a government official's honesty. Lum explains:

> There have been many attempts to explain the sig-
> nificance of this ball. Some think that it is a pearl
> possessed of great magical power which the dragon
> is trying to add to its treasure store, but if that is so
> there seems no particular reason why all dragons
> everywhere should be reaching in vainly for the

same treasure. . . . Yet another theory suggests that the pearl is the sun and the dragon is trying to swallow it. Try as he may, he will never succeed. For this reason the image of the dragon and the ball was supposedly originally painted on the screens at the gates of the magistrate and other governmental officials, the idea being that it was impossible for an official to be corrupt or unjust as it was for the dragon to swallow the sun.[47]

Yet, primarily because scholars have noted the similarities between Indian mythology and the Eastern dragon, the most likely answer is that the ball represents the moon. In Indian mythology, Indra seeks to swallow the moon to allow the release of the rains from the sky. Likewise, scholars attest, the dragon is probably chasing the moon to cause the storms for which it was noted. As Lum says:

> A more likely explanation is that the pearl represents the moon. The constellation of the dragon is one of the four major constellations which are used in Chinese astrology to indicate the four seasons, and it is the appearance of the moon just before the rising of the Dragon stars [the constellation of the dragon] that announces the coming of the Chinese New Year; thus the time when the moon is just out of reach of the dragon's claws is the time of spring and of new life, a symbol of hope.[48]

Or, as Smith concludes, "This seems to clear away any doubt as to the significance of the ball. It is the pearl-moon, which is both swallowed and vomited by the dragon."[49]

Certainly this connection between the moon and the Eastern dragon makes a good deal of sense because Indian mythology was carried to China by Buddhists who journeyed there from India; the myths included the concept of dragons, spiritual beings thought to be half human and half serpent. Called Nâgas, these beings were the Buddhist incarnation of the older Indian belief in Indra and Vritra. Not only did the Nâgas represent the power and force of water, but they also behaved like the dragon kings of Eastern dragon lore: Both watched over humankind while also controlling the waters of the world.

Even though some scholars argue that the Indian-Buddhist Nâgas explain the behavior of the Eastern dragon, there are problems with this explanation because it is incomplete. Certainly it seems likely that the Eastern dragon gained most of its personality and spiritual nature from the Nâga, but the image of the Eastern dragon actually already existed for as many as two thousand years before the arrival of the Indian Nâga in China. Thus, scholars are left to wonder from where the initial dragon images arose. One possibility is that the Chinese had already been influenced by the religions of India before its later adoption of the Nâga, although no one can say this for sure. In the end, as in the West, the precise tale of the origin of the Eastern dragon may never be known.

A pillar at the Temple of Confucius in China shows a dragon pawing a ball.

Could the Dragon Have Existed?

Almost all modern scholars agree that the dragon could not have existed, citing lack of archaeological evidence as well as the physical impossibilities of such a creature.

Some dragon specialists, however, do not agree with this conclusion. In fact, Peter Dickinson argues that there is as much evidence for the dragon's actual existence as there is for its impossibility.

In the pursuit of physical evidence of the dragon, scholars have pointed to cases in which individuals have claimed that the creature once existed. One of the most well known accounts appears in Pliny's *Natural History*. As Evans summarizes: "Pliny . . . refers to the "well-known case" of a 120-foot-long dragon killed . . . whose skin and jaws were exhibited in Rome for years afterward."[50]

Yet, given that no such evidence has been discovered in modern times, the testaments of writers like Pliny—and indeed like so many of the West and East—cannot be taken as fact. In an effort to explain how or why such testimonies might exist, some scholars suggest that ancient cultures stumbled across dinosaur bones, which they interpreted as the remains of dragons. Others contend that large lizards like the Komodo dragon or massive snakes like the anaconda were simply exaggerated from either fear or the need for dramatic effect, or both. Regardless, in almost all cases, scholars tend to agree that the variety and popularity of dragons throughout history is at least in part because the dragon never existed. Evans explains:

> Dragons we must remember are imaginary creatures, and the possibility of free variation exists here more readily than in the representation of concepts found in the natural realm. This is probably why the dragon has been so widely circulated between and within such different cultures: it is an extremely adaptable concept, drawing upon the seemingly universal fear (and sometimes respect) for snakes and serpents as well as on the special mythic needs of particular cultures in various geographical regions and periods of history.[51]

Therefore, historians, for the most part, have concluded that the dragon has always been an invention of the human imagination.

The Komodo dragon, a large lizard found in Indonesia, reveals its forked tongue.

As further evidence of this, scholars point to the physical impossibilities of such a fantastic animal. First, they argue, no beast known to humankind has been able to breathe fire. Second, no beast as large as a dragon could possibly fly. To prove the first point, scholars needed only to point out that an animal that breathed fire would have to be able to produce or generate that fire somewhere in its innards. This is, they argue, physiologically impossible. With regard to flying, it would be infeasible for a creature the size of a dragon to fly because of its aerodynamic constraints. Indeed, for a creature the size of a dragon to fly, its wingspan would need to be *more than six hundred feet wide*, and even then the dragon would be able to do little more than glide. Yet dragons are always described as having much smaller wings—or no wings at all in the case of the Eastern variety—and as being agile and quick fliers.

The Symbol of the Dragon

Not everyone agrees with the premise that dragons are strictly make-believe, however. Dickinson offers a counterargument in his book *The Flight of Dragons*. He states in his introduction: "I am not going to prove that ninety-foot lizards once floated in the skies of earth and scorched whole villages with plumes of flame, because I don't think it can be proved. . . . But I can put together a coherent theory which is at least as probable as the theory that dragons are completely legendary."[52] Dickinson offers a theory suggesting that dragons could have indeed existed and flown based on the idea that their bodies—much like that of a blimp or, more precisely, a dirigible (a larger and more flammable blimp filled with hydrogen)—were filled with gas that the dragon burned off periodically via its mouth. Most serious scholars, though, require more than simple conjecture to prove the dragon's existence. What they require is physical evidence. And despite his theories, Dickinson has been unable to produce that.

Perhaps of greater consequence to contemporary culture is not whether or not the dragon existed, but that the idea of the dragon has profoundly affected cultural and world history. Even today, the image of the dragon is readily used. On almost every continent in the world, paper dragons clog the street on Chinese New Year. Eastern art and architecture still use the dragon for its symbolic and cultural value. In the West, heraldic symbols of European

royalty still contain the image of the dragon. And modern literature and film continue to bring the dragon to life within the human imagination. Indeed, although the dragon itself may never have lived, it is most certainly still alive—at least within existing cultures and therefore within humanity as a whole.

A hot air baloon in the shape of a dragon symbolizes the ongoing human fascination with dragons.

Notes

Introduction: Of Might and Mystery

1. Grafton Elliot Smith, *The Evolution of the Dragon*. Manchester, England: The University Press; London and New York: Longmans, 1919, pp. 81–82.

Chapter One: What Is the Dragon?

2. *Beowulf.* Trans. David Wright. Harmondsworth, England: Penguin Classics, 1957, pp. 81–82.
3. Peter Lum, "Eastern Dragons," in *Fabulous Beasts*. New York: Pantheon, 1951, p. 117.
4. John Andrew Boyle, "Historical Dragon-Slayers," *Animals in Folklore*, Eds. J.R. Porter and W. M.S. Russell. Cambridge, England: D.S. Brewer, 1978, pp. 26–27.
5. Boyle, "Historical Dragon-Slayers," p. 27.
6. Boyle, "Historical Dragon-Slayers," p. 30.
7. Lum, "Eastern Dragons," p. 121.
8. Boyle, "Historical Dragon-Slayers," p. 24.
9. *Beowulf*, p. 92.
10. Lum, "Eastern Dragons," p. 112.
11. Ovid (Publius Ovidius Naso), *Metamorphoses*. Trans. Mary M. Innes. Harmondsworth, England: Penguin Classics, 1955, p. 148.

Chapter Two: To Slay a Dragon

12. A. R. Hope Moncrieff, *Romance and Legend of Chivalry*. New York: William H. Wise, 1934, p. 222.

13. Quoted in Jonathon D. Evans, "The Dragon," in *Mythical and Fabulous Creatures*. Ed. Malcolm South. New York: Greenwood, 1987, p. 39.
14. Moncrieff, *Romance and Legend of Chivalry*, p. 400.
15. Boyle, "Historical Dragon-Slayers," p. 23.
16. Thomas Bulfinch, *Bulfinch's Mythology*. New York: Thomas Y. Crowell 1962, p. 118.
17. Bulfinch, *Bulfinch's Mythology*, p. 119.
18. *Beowulf*, p. 90.
19. Moncrieff, *Romance and Legend of Chivalry*, pp. 222–23.
20. Evans, "The Dragon," p. 42.
21. Moncrieff, *Romance and Legend of Chivalry*, p. 401.
22. Moncrieff, *Romance and Legend of Chivalry*, pp. 402–403.
23. Helen Waddell, *Beasts and Saints*. London: Constable, 1953, p. 23.
24. Quoted in Boyle, "Historical Dragon-Slayers," p. 29.
25. Quoted in Boyle, "Historical Dragon-Slayers," pp. 29–30.
26. Boyle, "Historical Dragon-Slayers," p. 31.

Chapter Three: The Wise Dragons of the East

27. Quoted in M.W. De Visser, *The Dragon in China and Japan* (Japan). Germany: Afdeeling Letterkunde, 1969, p. 70.

28. Quoted in De Visser, *The Dragon in China and Japan*, p. 70.
29. Quoted in De Visser, *The Dragon in China and Japan*, p. 112.
30. Lum, "Eastern Dragons," p. 115.
31. De Visser, *The Dragon in China and Japan*, p. 134.
32. Lum, "Eastern Dragons," p. 120.
33. Quoted in De Visser, *The Dragon in China and Japan*, p. 63.
34. Quoted in De Visser, *The Dragon in China and Japan*, p. 220.
35. Quoted in De Visser, *The Dragon in China and Japan*, p. 39.
36. De Visser, *The Dragon in China and Japan*, p. 123.
37. Lum, "Eastern Dragons," pp. 114–15.

Chapter Four: Origins of the Dragon
38. Smith, *The Evolution of the Dragon*, p. 80.
39. Smith, *The Evolution of the Dragon*, p. 80.

40. Evans, "The Dragon," p. 31.
41. Arthur Cotterell, *A Dictionary of World Mythology*. Oxford: Oxford UP, 1986, p. 54.
42. Cotterell, *A Dictionary of World Mythology*, p. 53.
43. Cotterell, *A Dictionary of World Mythology*, p. 54.
44. F.G. Holweck, *A Biographical Dictionary of the Saints*. Binghamton, New York: Vail-Ballou Press, 1924.
45. Evans, "The Dragon," p. 31.
46. Quoted in Smith, *The Evolution of the Dragon*, p. 101.
47. Lum, "Eastern Dragons," p. 113.
48. Lum, "Eastern Dragons," p. 113.
49. Smith, *The Evolution of the Dragon*, p. 101.
50. Evans, "The Dragon," p. 38.
51. Evans, "The Dragon," p. 28.
52. Peter Dickinson, *The Flight of Dragons*. London: Pierrot, 1979, p. 1.

For Further Reading

Graeme Base, *The Discovery of Dragons*. New York: Harry N. Abrams, 1996. Ostensibly real-life adventures about dragons as told by the adventurers themselves through letters and documents. Includes tales by a Viking explorer, a Chinese female merchant, and a Prussian cartographer.

Beowulf: A New Verse Translation. Trans. Seamus Heaney. New York: Farrar, Straus and Giroux, 2000. A profound and moving new translation by acclaimed Nobel Prize–winning Irish poet Seamus Heaney, in which the wonder of the Old English original is made accessible to all.

Michael Hague, *The Book of Dragons*. New York: William Morrow, 1995. This book has seventeen classic dragon tales, such as J. R. R. Tolkien's "Bilbo Baggins and the Smaug," and William H. G. Kingston's "St. George and the Dragon." The stories are illustrated in black and white and in watercolors.

Ernest Ingersoll, *Dragons and Dragon Lore*. Detroit: Singing Tree Press, 1968. This book is filled with stories and information about dragons from a variety of traditions and cultures.

David E. Jones, *An Instinct for Dragons*. New York: Routledge, 2000. Many societies have a concept of and a word for the dragon, even though the creature apparently never existed. Dr. David Jones proposes that the concept may have derived from ancestral humans' fears of three kinds of predators.

Anne McCaffrey, *Dragonriders of Pern*. Garden City, NY: Nelson Doubleday, 1978. Anne McCaffrey's Pern is one of the most memorable worlds in dragon fantasy literature. Humans and their flying dragon companions live in fear of "thread," a periodic threat which the dragons are needed to combat. This edition contains the first three novels: *Dragonflight*, *Dragonquest*, and *The White Dragon*.

Works Consulted

Beowulf. Trans. David Wright. Harmondsworth, England: Penguin Classics, 1957. One of the definitive prose translations of this classic Old English work.

John Andrew Boyle, "Historical Dragon-Slayers," in *Animals in Folklore*. Ed. J. R. Porter and W. M. S. Russell. Cambridge, England: D. S. Brewer, 1978. A scholarly investigation of those historical persons who were claimed to have been involved with the dragon. Boyle looks at historical figures as both demiurge and rain god.

Thomas Bulfinch, *Bulfinch's Mythology*. New York: Thomas Y. Crowell, 1962. The complete collection of ancient mythologies is by one of the most renowned mythologians of our time.

Arthur Cotterell, *A Dictionary of World Mythology*. Oxford: Oxford UP, 1986. The complete Oxford dictionary covers dozens of mythologies and hundreds of mythological deities and demigods.

M. W. De Visser, *The Dragon in China and Japan*. Germany: Afdeeling Letterkunde, 1969. One of the seminal works on the Eastern dragon's development and surrounding myths. This book is one of the few that includes the original Eastern texts in precise translations.

Peter Dickinson, *The Flight of Dragons*. London: Pierrot, 1979. A unique book that criticizes current scholarship for failing to accept the possibility of dragons while also putting forward a comprehensive theory that might allow for their actual existence.

Jonathon D. Evans, "The Dragon," in *Mythical and Fabulous Creatures*. Ed. Malcolm South. New York: Greenwood, 1987. A comprehensive and knowledgeable overview of the primary scholarship completed on the subject of dragons.

F. G. Holweck, *A Biographical Dictionary of the Saints*. Binghamton, NY: Vail-Ballou Press, 1924. An index of the Catholic saints accompanied by brief descriptions of their actual lives.

Peter Lum, "Eastern Dragons," in *Fabulous Beasts*. New York: Pantheon, 1951. Lum provides a strong introduction to Eastern and Western dragons, while also wonderfully retelling some of the best-known and important myths involving the dragon.

A. R. Hope Moncrieff, *Romance and Legend of Chivalry*. New York: William H. Wise, 1934. Primarily a work on the chivalric legends, the author provides a comprehensive picture of how the dragon fit into the medieval romance.

Ovid (Publius Ovidius Naso), *Metamorphoses*. Trans. Mary M. Innes. Harmondsworth, England: Penguin Classics, 1955. The definitive translation of one of the most famous Romans and storytellers of all time.

Grafton Elliot Smith, *The Evolution of the Dragon*. Manchester, England: The University Press; London and New York: Longmans, 1919. A superior scholarly look at the origin of the dragon and how it evolved in both Western and Eastern cultures.

J. R. R. Tolkien, *The Hobbit*. London: Allen and Unwin, 1937. Tolkien's first fictive venture into the realm of Middle Earth in which the hobbit, Bilbo, is recruited by the dwarves to steal treasure from the terrible dragon, Smaug.

Helen Waddell, *Beasts and Saints*. London: Constable, 1953. An overview of canonical and apocryphal saints associated with a variety of beasts, both real and imaginary.

Index

Picture Credits

About the Author

Michael J. Wyly received his Master of Fine Arts in creative writing from California State University, Long Beach, where he is an instructor of English literature and language. He has also functioned as a fiction and poetry editor for several small-press publications. Wyly is currently on sabbatical from his teaching duties and lives and writes in Paris, France.